MAN & WOMAN
JOY IN ONENESS

ESTER RASBAND

Deseret Book Company
Salt Lake City, Utah

© 1982 Deseret Book Company
All rights reserved
Printed in the United States of America
First printing April 1982

ISBN 0-87747-917-8
Library of Congress Catalog Card Number 82-70997

To our sons, Jim and Win,
and their someday wives,
with a prayer for their
eternal oneness.

I am woman.
If there is pride in man, there is pride in me,
For I am part of him.
I am his partner, his energy, his heart.
I am none the less when you call us *man*.
That is the name of us,
And we are one.

If either of us treasures any separateness,
Looks to the part and not the whole,
The soul of all eternity is sacrificed—
For joy in oneness is the godlike role.

Contents

1	Principles of Partnership	1
2	Eliminating the Adversary Relationship	6
3	Becoming a Worthy Partner	14
4	Working in Unity	19
5	Finding Fulfillment	22
6	Achieving Family Goals	26
7	Learning to Compromise	33
8	Seeking the Good	41
9	Loving When Alone	45
10	The Joy in Oneness	48
	Index	51

1

Principles of Partnership

I am a woman. Driven by my generation to examine my role, I have asked questions about fulfillment. I have found answers about joy. With the help of the Holy Ghost, I am beginning to understand what the prophet Lehi called our reason for being.

I have long known that my marriage is the key to what my soul craves, but I know, too, that many women will not marry in this life. I had been tempted to believe that they had a different purpose—the potential for separate fulfillment.

But from my search for understanding, I have learned what the Savior has made abundantly clear: that all of us have the same purpose, and it is not separateness. Man or woman, married or single, we are to become one with our Father in Heaven—partners in purpose.

When we pledge this partnership, we call it

"consecration," and that means we will put the purposes of the kingdom of God above our own desires until, finally, the purposes of the Kingdom become our own. When our desires are the same, when our love is complete, that is oneness.

This partnership, this oneness, is what we were placed on earth to learn, because it is joy.

Through the ages, as some have caught little glimpses of this completeness, they have tried to express their insight so that others could understand it. The pages of our literature are filled with this ardent effort.

"No man is an island," said John Donne, and now three hundred years later I know what he knew, feel what he felt.

Alexander Pope understood, and he said, "All are but parts of one stupendous whole, / Whose body Nature is, and God the soul." (*An Essay on Man*, Epistle I, l. 267.)

Now two hundred years later, I thrill with him to see "where faith, law, morals all began, / All end in love of God and love of man." And I take comfort that some in my own generation also understand, like Pierre Teilhard De Chardin, who in 1955 said, "If there were no internal propensity to unite, even at a prodigiously rudimentary level—indeed, in the very molecule itself—it would be physically impossible for love to appear higher up. . . . Driven by the forces of love, the fragments of the world seek each other so that the world may come into being."

But even in the face of all these insights, I have to ask myself why each of us seems to have to discover oneness for himself. Nowhere has it been expressed with such clarity as it was by Paul when he said that man is *nothing* unless he has love, which never seeks its own interests. (1 Corinthians 13:2, 5.) And nowhere has it been expressed with such beauty and love as when the Savior prayed, "Holy Father, keep through thine own name those whom thou hast given me, that they may be one, as we are." (John 17:11.)

It is so deeply thrilling to know how dearly he wanted that joy for us. He showed us, taught us, and died for us that we might achieve that joy:

> Master, which is the great commandment in the law?
> Jesus said unto him, Thou shalt love the Lord thy God with all thy heart, and with all thy soul, and with all thy mind. This is the first and great commandment. And the second is like unto it, Thou shalt love thy neighbour as thyself. (Matthew 22:36-39.)

With those two commandments, the Savior helped us to see that the principles of partnership are the same whether we are partners with man or with God, and that we must use this life to learn them. King Benjamin explained, "When ye are in the service of your fellow beings ye are only in the service of your God." (Mosiah 2:17.)

On these principles of partnership (love and service) hang all the law and the prophets.

They are difficult to learn. They are lessons that we often would rather withdraw from. But God gives us marriage, and it becomes necessary to learn them, because in family life we either experience the joy of oneness, or we are in misery. It is not difficult to understand why families exist only in the celestial kingdom; surely oneness is a celestial state, and without oneness family life is not desirable—or even tolerable. Having families on earth might well be termed trial celestialization.

Because the principles of partnership can be painful to learn, it is now fashionable for married couples to try to eliminate this pain by rejecting those principles. They have no children—or else make arrangements so the children interfere as little as possible with their separate lives. They try to make few demands on each other and carefully guard their right to refuse to give. It is not really family life.

My single sisters and brothers, too, may find it very attractive to reject these painful lessons, and indeed it is much easier to withdraw from them single than married.

Principles of Partnership

Married or single, there is an absence of joy if we reject oneness with others and therefore with God. When we settle for this life that seems simpler, we have a counterfeit peace.

With desire, and with faith, the principles of partnership can be learned, whether we are married or single, male or female. The joy that man exists to feel comes to us when we leave off our separateness. It is the joy in oneness.

2

Eliminating the Adversary Relationship

Recently I taught a seminary class that tended to divide itself quite naturally into groups. These groups became our "zones" for competition in scripture chase. As in most seminary classes, two or three students were more talented in competition than the others, and the contest was most intense between the two groups that had these specially talented ones. The members of one of the groups sat very close to each other in a tight circle. The boy who knew all the answers quickly gave the page numbers to the other members of the group and helped each one of them find the scriptures before he raised his hand. Almost always his team won.

A rival team sat apart, and the talented boy raised his hand instantly when he found the scripture and got upset with his teammates for not making more of an effort to win.

"It isn't fair," he said. "My team won't try. I'm

Eliminating the Adversary Relationship

the only one on my team that knows the answers!"

I pointed out to him that there was no rule against giving his team members the answer and suggested that he try it. So on the next round he sat in his chair and said, "Hey you guys, get over here and get the answer. Get over here! Get over here!" But the round was over, and they lost again.

I said, "You know, if the mountain won't go to Mohammed, Mohammed may have to go to the mountain."

He responded, "I'm the one that knows the answers—I'm not going to go running over there to *them*." And they lost the next round, too.

Finally I told them the secret: "Look you guys —move in really close together so that no time is lost communicating. The closer you get together, the more apt you are to win." There was some grumbling about who would do the moving and about "fairness." Each of them moved his chair a token inch or two and sneered at the others.

But on the other side of the room an interesting thing was happening. The winning group was listening to my counsel and moving their chairs even closer together. In the next round they had record time, and the other group still had no chance at all. They rarely even took second place. They simply refused to eliminate their adversary relationship. The fight among themselves was more important to them than winning as a team. I finally found that I had to abandon having teams, not because the students learned more working alone, but because not every one in the class seemed ready for the higher law.

When we become defensive trying not to be taken advantage of, we often settle for less than we could learn, less than we could be. In addition, we forfeit winning the big one: the joy in oneness.

A few years ago as stake Young Women's president, I felt deeply that a certain young woman should join our committee. She was greatly talented, and we needed her. The stake presidency made the call, and she attended her first meeting. We did some brainstorming about a theme for an upcoming leadership meeting that would include the Aaronic Priesthood committee. I was pleased with the results. A meeting with the men was to follow that meeting, and I said, "We'll submit this for approval to the men in the next meeting, but I'll go ahead and make assignments now, so that we'll be organized and ready to go."

Our new committee member responded defensively: "What are the *men* going to do? It sounds like this is going to be just like every other time I've worked with men. The women do all the work."

The rest of us sort of smiled. And I said as quietly as I could, "If we do for the Aaronic Priesthood

Eliminating the Adversary Relationship

committee what we do best, they will do for us what they do best. Some of these creative things are the kinds of things they won't even see. They're almost feminine things, and we're in a better position to do them. If we do it with love, they will serve us with love, too."

Well, she did not say much. Something like "Harumph." Her adversary relationship was difficult for her to give up. But this sister struggled with her separateness, and a year or so later when we were all released she said to me, "Do you know what the unique experience of working on this board has been? It's been *love*. I've never felt such love. Everyone wanted to serve each other. And I've never before worked with priesthood holders who made me feel like a queen. To think of sitting in meetings with high councilors and a member of the stake presidency and having them make me feel so important."

My young friend felt important because she *was* important; she had made herself important by giving, by making herself a partner. By not treasuring her separateness and guarding against giving too much, she had felt the giving response of others. The love she was experiencing was the joy of oneness.

This most effective tool that Satan has to keep us from oneness—this adversary relationship—is being intensely peddled in our time. We must be ever so careful not to buy it. Women are being told how downtrodden they are, and like a perfectly healthy person who is told she looks pale, we rush to the mirror and let the color drain from our faces.

Self-pity is reaching epidemic proportions. A defensive ugliness is rising up between people who love each other and have pledged to become one flesh.

Women everywhere are catching the disease. Even those who disavow the movement are finding themselves "picked on." Marriages are being damaged or destroyed, and couples are not feeling the joy of oneness.

Self-pity is a destructive force at all levels, not just within marriage. Several months ago I was visiting Williamsburg. There was no tour guide at the Bruton Parish Church, but a young costumed lad was available to answer questions. He was in high spirits and was volunteering a good deal of history without being asked. He was very knowledgeable, and the tour was most enjoyable. He started to talk about the seating arrangements. The men, he said, sat on one side of the aisle, and the women on the other. "And in the box," he pointed, "sat the faculty from William and Mary College."

A young woman who had been standing there for some time asked, "Why was the faculty in the box?"

ELIMINATING THE ADVERSARY RELATIONSHIP

His answer was brief and given with a smile. "Because they were considered clergy."

"Oh, I see," she said. And then her eyes and lips narrowed. "At least it wasn't because they were looking down on them like they were over here at the second class citizens on this side of the aisle."

Her remark was hostile, defensive, and a sign of self-pity.

The young man became quiet. Then he said, "No, I'm sure the reasons weren't the same." He turned around and walked away from us. All the partnership was lost between that man and that woman. Things she might have learned were lost to her (and to me) because she had adopted an adversary relationship. They were no longer a team learning about the Bruton Parish Church. They were adversaries, and he withdrew. She turned to her little guide book—to the lesser law of working alone.

The unfortunate young woman was responding to what has come to be called "consciousness raising" about the "plight" of women. Do not let society raise your consciousness to a new depth of self-pity. Nobody can put you down but you.

Another way that the adversary relationship is being peddled in our world is by making service a dirty word. "Spend your life serving," they say, "and where does it get you? Nowhere!" And then the tirade continues. "Why, I've done nothing but play doormat for my family. I've scrubbed floors, washed, ironed, mended, cooked, waited on them hand and foot! I've spent my whole life in service, and does anyone appreciate it? No!"

I am always tempted, and sometimes driven, to say, "Hey, what you're describing is some sort of dirty word, it's true. But that's not service! To have served them would have been to teach them to do those things for themselves. Service would have been to make them self-sufficient through participation. Can you really call it a service to have made them so dependent on you that they can't function? No, that may be a dirty word all right, but it's not service!"

I wish that I had not forgotten the name of the brilliant person who said, "Mothers are not for leaning on, they are for making leaning unnecessary."

Many women set up the adversary relationship in their would-be partnership by being *used* instead of *useful*. This is a common error, and servitude *is* a dirty word. But please, be careful not to call it service. Service is something that happens in oneness. It is serving the best interests of each other in response to purposes and goals of the partnership. Service is the kind of thing we do when we reach to be one with our Father in heaven. It always brings joy. When we use the resources at our command—our talents, our time, our love—to do those things

Eliminating the Adversary Relationship

that only we can do in pursuance of our shared goals and purposes, then that is service. Service is not a dirty word, but it is not surprising that Satan should try to make it sound like one, because service is the surest way to eliminate his most useful tool, the adversary relationship.

3

Becoming a Worthy Partner

Once after I had discussed oneness during a Church meeting, a good friend approached me and said, "Ester, that's not the way it is at all. I attended a meeting just the other day where a General Authority said that the individual comes first, then the family, then the Church, and then the rest of the world. You first have to be fulfilled yourself."

I think she made up that last part herself. That priority list has to do with responsibility. We are responsible for our own salvation first, for our own welfare first. I feel sure that no General Authority ever said we are responsible for "finding" ourselves first, or for "turning ourselves on" first. As far as "fulfillment" is concerned, I am confident the General Authority would have told my friend that fulfillment comes through service, and that when we seek more than our worthiness and well-being before we reach out to the rest of the world, we may never be fulfilled at all. For instance, Elder George Albert Smith said, "It is not what we receive that enriches our lives, it is what we give." (*Conference Report,* April 1935, p. 46.)

I wonder how many people, trying to find themselves first, never find themselves at all. I wonder how many think of service as a "next step," and so become paralyzed in separateness, never knowing the joy in oneness.

The partnership our souls crave with our mates, with others, and with God, requires worthy partners. If service is the end of our being, then surely we must strive to make our service valuable.

That means that women who are able should have an education—not just in home-related subjects, but in all areas. Remember, the culture in their homes will be limited to what they know. They should have the rest and relaxation to keep themselves renewed. They should have the recreation to keep their spirits light, because they are usually the mood-setting partners. They should maintain the physical health to keep the vitality that their role requires. In short, they should not "seek their own," but they should ever be alert to the kind of self they are offering. They should be worthy partners.

Likewise, a man's education should not stop at learning to make a living. There is more to his role than that. He, too, needs the rest, recreation, and physical attention to maintain his energy. In addition, he will probably need some fix-it skills, some cultural appreciation, and some skills in human relationships.

Single people may need some different skills, but the concept is the same: their first responsibility is to themselves to become worthy contributors to the oneness that will be their joy. Married or single, man or woman, finding oneself is not the issue—the issue is having a better self to lose in service.

It is a natural corollary that we must respect each other's efforts at growth. A few weeks ago I was disturbed by some conversation in our home. Some good friends were undergoing a difficult financial decision about the education of their children. They felt they didn't have enough money for tuition for both their boy and their girl. They hit upon what I considered to be a brilliant solution: both children would work during the summer to earn half the tuition so that both could go.

My sons sat around my table, and one of them said, "Well, it doesn't really matter for the girl; she'll only be a mother anyway. She doesn't need an education."

In the interest of good feelings I restrained myself from saying, "Look you jokers, who sits up at night and helps you with your homework? Where would *you* be without *my* education?" Instead, I simply smiled and quoted Brigham Young: "Educate a man and you educate a man. Educate a woman and you educate a family."

And I thought about a quotation from dear Phyllis McGinley: "To what barbarian plane have we descended when an education is worth only what it will bring in the marketplace?"

It is true, I know, that a man's vocational education must take a great deal of priority in any marriage, but both partners should be willing to give a great deal as well to their other needs.

I am afraid that parents are not raising their sons to understand the importance of a woman's contribution and the necessity for her to prepare to make it. Also, I fear that they stress church and work roles to such a degree that they do not teach them to be husbands.

We must teach our boys to be good husbands. We should help them understand what kind of girls to look for and how to be worthy of them. For the most part, girls are what they are to be attractive to boys. An old song is based on this principle:

> He likes to bill and coo,
> I never liked to bill and coo,
> But he likes to bill and coo,
> And that's my weakness now.

I often hear from my sons how important it is to

them to have a "bright" wife, and how dull it is to be with a "dumb" girl. How ironic that they should not see the need for these "bright" wives to have a good education. This reminds me of some boys who made disparaging remarks about "unfeminine" girls as they came back from backpacking. Many girls never learn to like outdoor activities because many boys do not find girls who participate in these activities attractive. Yet some of these same boys will grow into men who lament the fact that their wives do not want to go camping and fishing with them. How sad that our boys, with their adolescent taste, *create* our young women, only later to bemoan the fact that they do not have the higher product. How sad that their fathers, who often look admiringly at the glamour of career women, have made their wives feel the need for recognition outside the home only later to bemoan the fact that their children have no mother.

If we want our young women to grow up to be strong, righteous wives, we must train our boys to value their worthiness, endorse their preparation, and treat them well.

Though the man presides over the marriage, both spouses must make great contributions, and the total contribution they make to the kingdom of God will be greater if they work together and respect the responsibility of each to be a worthy partner.

4

Working in Unity

Over the years I have identified an attitude I call "employee mentality." The person who suffers with this attitude (and I use the word *suffer* as an antonym for *joy*) will never rise to management level unless he changes his vision.

Seeing ourselves in a certain light will always limit us to that light, because maintaining that light becomes our purpose. It is sometimes easier to see this on an eternal level than on a day-to-day basis. Unless we see ourselves as children of God, we will limit ourselves to mortal purposes. But if we, understanding our birthright, see ourselves as potential gods, we will adjust our activities to meet that vision. In other words, we cannot expect to become gods if we do not adopt a mentality of godliness.

I have a well-educated friend who wants to join the management of the company for which he works. He hates telling people he is a "nobody." He craves recognition and remuneration. He resents his bosses and thinks they take advantage of him. When they ask him to stay a few minutes past five, he complains mightily and puts an extra hour on his time card. If somehow he has sick leave left over at the end of the year, he suddenly develops some reason to stay home in bed so he can get "what's coming to him." Those of us who spend time with him are always hearing that "they" ask him to do things that are "not his job." "I'm not being paid for that," he says, "and I'm not going to do it."

It is an oft-sung tune he is singing, and I always wish for those who sing it that they had heard the more lofty notes of my mother, who sent her children out into the work force with this rewarding secret: "Always do only what you are paid for, and you will always be paid only for what you do."

My mother's familiar song was just another way to say: see yourself as an employee, limit yourself to employee purposes, and you will never be a manager.

It is interesting that the "employee mentality" almost always is hostile, a prime example of the adversary relationship. Refusing to be one with an employer has obvious parallels to refusing to be one with God. Both are limiting.

Sometimes the problem is obedience—"My creativity and freedom are being stifled!" Sometimes it is being asked to give too much—"They must think they own me!" "That's not my responsibility! I'm not getting paid for that!" Sometimes it is support for an immediate supervisor—"Who does he think he is?" and sometimes it is the challenge of fellow workers —"If I have to work with that idiot . . ."

The cries you have heard at home and at church are the same you have heard at work, and the temporal consequences at work will parallel the eternal consequences of withholding oneself at home and church.

We can have almost anything we are willing to pay the price for. If we see ourselves in a role clearly enough to accept the purposes of that role, to work in unity and harmony with those purposes, the role will be ours, not as a reward, but as a reality.

I envision a world where starting salaries are unimportant and goals more important than prestige, where people do not need to "fight the system." There are abuses within the system, but when we find them, let it not be because our employee mentality created them.

Lofty goals require lofty effort. Let not defensive pettiness stand in the way of our achievement. Dante warned, "O human race, born to fly upward, wherefore at a little wind dost thou so fall?"

Let us accept each other's purposes in love and dedication, and work together to bring them about.

5

Finding Fulfillment

Fulfillment is the delight that people expect to feel when they "find themselves." Indeed, I believe that is precisely when they will feel it—when they have lost themselves enough to find themselves.

Fulfillment is often accompanied by recognition. If you will ask successful people how they got that way, you will find that very few of them will say, "I wanted to find something that made me feel good" or "I wanted recognition." Most of the happy ones will say, "I had a goal I wanted to accomplish."

My husband is involved in several things that bring him a lot of recognition. He is a quiet man who does not seek praise. But, as he says, he "backs into it." He sees needs to be filled and starts trying to fill them. Before long he is president of an organization or director of a company or in whatever position he needs to be in to reach his goals.

For a long time, our ward didn't have much of a

Scouting program. My husband was an Eagle Scout and loved Scouting, so he got involved. When it was time for Scout camp, he took a week's vacation and went to camp so that our boys could go. He invited groups of boys to our home to work on merit badges with our sons, and quietly encouraged boys to advance. He badly wanted Scouting for our sons and for the other boys in our ward.

Well, bishops are very quick. It did not take long at all until he was called as Scoutmaster. He hesitated to take the position because the demands on his time were already great. But getting Scouting for those boys was so important to him that he could not refuse. At the end of his three years as Scoutmaster, he was thrilled with his boys. He had good relationships with all of the boys in the ward—not just the Boy Scouts. One of his Eagle Scouts barely got in under the wire; he had his Eagle Scout court after his eighteenth birthday. A priest told him that he had chosen his life's work as a result of time spent with my husband in his truck on the way to a Scout activity.

When we went to the Boy Scout recognition dinner, we had more Eagle Scouts than anyone else in our council. My husband kept making trips to the podium, getting awards for all the things he had done.

And there were those who said, "I'd like to be a Scoutmaster like that! How'd you do it?"

MAN AND WOMAN: JOY IN ONENESS

His answer: "I didn't really want to be a Scoutmaster, I just backed into it. I just wanted the boys to have Scouting, and so I got involved, and . . . "

I believe we will not find fulfillment by wanting to walk up to the awards desk. Although it is possible to get the recognition with that motivation, we will not find *fulfillment* except by wanting to contribute. Neither will we find purpose. Neither will we find oneness with our Father in heaven, which is the only complete joy we will ever know.

We tend to think of activities instead of goals, but any time that means become ends in themselves, we are in trouble.

There are so many people who cannot decide what to do with their lives because they are trying to find what "turns them on." They are looking for a means to provide sustained excitement. The excitement is the only end they have in view.

I know of no one who can sustain a level of excitement from an activity. Fulfillment comes only from wanting something so much you are willing to invest yourself in achieving it. Then, seeing it happen is exciting.

I got my college education after my children had already been born. I knew that I wanted to study something that would enrich my motherhood. I chose English and greatly enjoyed my studies. But I was not *fulfilled* by them until one night when I sat up until about one o'clock in the morning with a son who had to write a paper on Shakespeare. He had not felt the beauty of Shakespeare in school, but that night he said, "Gosh, Mom, it's super, isn't it?"

Now *that's* fulfillment!

Examine your motivation. If the activities in your life are ends in themselves, I can almost promise you a lifetime of restlessness, emptiness, and separateness. But if you are working hard to make something happen in your world, something righteous and worthwhile, then its achievement will bring real fulfillment to your life.

6

Achieving Family Goals

A few years ago I substitute taught a Relief Society class on self-esteem. We started talking about achieving self-esteem through using our talents in service, and the response I got from the sisters bewildered me. Here is a sample: "That doesn't build self-esteem! That's just a way to make me feel inadequate and miserable. On Tuesdays when I teach my Primary class, the house is a mess, I don't get the laundry done, and dinner is just thrown together. My husband gets upset with me—and that's no way to feel good about myself." Others chimed in with "Sounds like home" and "Isn't it the truth!"

At first I grinned defensively. "I guess my standards are lower," I said. "If I taught Primary, Tuesday night would be McDonald's night, or TV dinners night, or soup and crackers night. And my kids would throw in a load of laundry for me. If the

Achieving Family Goals

house is a mess for a day or so—big deal! It was a good Primary class!"

Most of the sisters were shocked.

"Do you really *do* that?"

"Oh yes," I said. "For a leadership meeting the house might be considerably less than perfect for a week or more."

Then the sisters started admitting that this happened in their homes, too, but that they could not feel good about it like I did.

"I just feel terribly guilty when I don't put my family first."

"Hey, wait a minute," I said. "We were married in the temple. In my home one of our chief family goals is to build the kingdom of God. Our family is a talent pool with which to fill our family goals. If there is a need that my talents will fill, then my entire family helps me fill that need. It might be that their contribution will be to eat TV dinners some nights, or do the laundry, or live in something less than House Beautiful for a while. Or it might even be more direct, like helping me make visual aids or brainstorm. But if I give, they have given. Our family oneness has made something good happen. If one of us has served, all of us have."

It was time for the other sisters to be bewildered. They reported that in most of their homes putting the family first meant that they could do other service only if everything was physically perfect at home, as if service were a privilege reserved for getting the chores done. No one else in their families felt any obligation to serve.

I was not talking about *consistent* chaos or neglect. Order in the home is always a top priority for people trying to live the gospel. But lasagne and chocolate cake are not always more important than a member of the family serving others. But some husbands sometimes think they are.

That night when I went home I put my arms around my husband. I told him, "You are wonderful. Thank you for helping me and taking pride in what I do; thank you for having me on your team and for being a member of mine."

Not long after that my husband and I attended a professional banquet. Another doctor was there without his wife. We asked about her, which led to this conversation:

"I'm so glad I married a nurse. Only a nurse could understand that she takes second place to medicine."

"Well, I'm not a nurse," I said, "and I don't have any problem. But then, neither do I feel second place." And then half playfully, I said, "Shame on you for making her feel that way!"

"Well, how could she feel any other way? She's second place and that's all there is to it! Let me tell you a story and see if you don't agree. Last Thursday night we had planned a big dinner party and just as the guests were all arriving, I got called to the hospital. I wasn't supposed to be on call, but it happened that the patient had a problem that only I could handle. So I left my wife at the dinner party and went off to play doctor. How could she feel anything but second place? She *is* second place."

I felt such sympathy for both of them in their separateness.

"Oh, I've been married to a doctor for more than twenty years," I smiled. "That's an old story. No doctor's wife escapes that kind of thing. But surely long ago you two decided that taking care of the sick took priority in your home. The night of your party, your family had two jobs to do—you took care of the one at the hospital, and she had to take care of the one at home. At the end of the evening you could get together and feel that with each other's support, you both made it."

He shook his head. "Medicine's mine, and the home is hers. If I'd have put her first, I'd have stayed home."

I changed the subject. Soon I found myself thinking about a night sixteen years earlier when my husband was a resident physician. There was a very sick woman at the hospital who was having a rough night, and she had no family at all. No one cared. My husband spent the night at the hospital sitting by her bed so that when she woke she would have support. The next morning she thanked him profusely and suggested that he, too, might be single. My husband told her that he had a wife and a little boy and that his wife was pregnant.

"Oh, no!" she said. "Your wife will never forgive me! Now you'll have to go home to a fight!"

Jim laughed. "My wife's happy to let me help you," he said. "I'm sure she's loved feeling that you are more comfortable."

My husband had called it right, of course, but I was only beginning to understand why she feared otherwise. The doctor at the party and the sisters at Relief Society were expressing the same thing—a separateness in their homes that created jealousies and anxieties. "Second place" only occurs when family goals take second priority, and surely the best way of seeing that does not happen is to know what those goals are.

A couple should write down their family goals before they marry. Each partner might make a list and then come together to combine the two. If the lists are too disparate, that may be a clue that the marriage would not be a good one.

A couple should revise their goals over the years and work to achieve them in priority order. There should never be "her" goals and "his" goals, only

ACHIEVING FAMILY GOALS

family goals to which all are committed. This does not rule out role differences; it only means that giving support in those roles should never be cause for distress. If all family members give their all, there should never be any separateness.

As we come closer to oneness, we will have less need for lists and written goals. The priorities will come from shared desires and will be obvious when support is needed.

Whenever I think of couples pulling together, I think of King Lamoni's wife. When Lamoni heard the gospel, he was overcome by the Spirit and fell to the earth as if dead for several days. The people wanted Lamoni's wife to bury him. But after checking with Lamoni's servants (and possibly through earlier communication with her husband) she knew of Lamoni's great confidence in Ammon. Because she wanted to further her husband's goals, she tried to understand what her husband would have her do, so she went to Ammon and asked his advice. Her love was rewarded with a witness of the Spirit that her husband was still alive. She brought many blessings to her family.

Now contrast her behavior with that of Lamoni's father's wife. Ever since his encounter with Ammon on the way to Middoni (when Ammon could have had half the kingdom in return for the king's life but asked only favors for others), Lamoni's father had been preoccupied with Ammon's message, so that when Ammon's brothers arrived he was a "golden contact." He became convinced of the truthfulness of the gospel, and he, too, fell to the earth. His wife either did not know or did not care what her husband had been seeking, and she ordered the death of the men who had brought him the gospel. Lamoni's father's servants knew the power of the missionaries, but his wife, thinking only of her own fright, would have prevailed in her desire had not her husband been raised up to convince her, too, of the truthfulness of the gospel. (See Alma 17-22.)

    A husband and wife should be aware of each other's goals and should make their goals known to each other. They should then share their goals with the entire family and work toward their goals as a family. This will make possible great achievement and therefore great fulfillment.

7

Learning to Compromise

I attended a June wedding performed by Elder David B. Haight in the Salt Lake Temple. "Today," he told the young bride and groom, "is the day that you become one, the day you blend your individual desires in mutual compromise."

Even assuming the great love that two people can have for each other, it is a rare couple that understands the principles of partnership from the outset. That beautiful stage in which priorities are automatically set by oneness with the Holy Ghost is not achieved overnight. It is, as a matter of fact, a forever project. Every couple has varying degrees of lingering separateness long after the commitment has been made to become one. But by not *treasuring* that separateness, and with a firm faith in eternal progression, a couple can move steadfastly toward the joy in oneness. This is done, as Elder Haight suggested, through mutual compromise.

Man and Woman: Joy in Oneness

There are many who think of compromise as something passive—as being acted upon instead of acting. They fear *being* compromised. But compromise occurs when two parties actively consider each other's goals and desires and lovingly agree upon what is best for the *unit* that they have become.

Woman follows man and man follows God in a chain of obedience. Both man and woman are followers. Neither is designed to submit to the will of the other. Together, they must seek to know and to do God's will. If they are both righteous enough, they will both understand his will through the power of the Holy Ghost. But that understanding comes line upon line, judgment upon judgment, loving compromise upon loving compromise.

President Spencer W. Kimball defines the role of the husband as "presiding" officer. (*BYU Speeches of the Year*, Sept. 1974, p. 237.) In business, partnerships often fail and have to be dissolved even when commercially successful. Corporations, on the other hand, rarely dissolve unless failing financially. This failure, it seems to me, is the absence of a "presiding officer" in a partnership. Fortunately that is not the case in the partnership we call marriage. The "president" of a marriage has the responsibility to evaluate goals and desires and lovingly implement the purposes of the "chairman of the board" (his Father in heaven) for the good of "the company" (the family).

LEARNING TO COMPROMISE

If he does a good job, he keeps his position (his priesthood) and gets regular pay raises (increases in joy). Sometimes the input is inadequate, and the choices are not always clear. The president's job is tough. He must bring to it "long-suffering, . . . gentleness and meekness, and . . . love unfeigned." (Doctrine and Covenants 121:41.) But the rewards are great: "The Holy Ghost shall be thy constant companion, and thy scepter an unchanging scepter of righteousness and truth; and thy dominion shall be an everlasting dominion, and *without compulsory means* it shall flow unto thee forever and ever." (Doctrine and Covenants 121:46; italics added.)

With the goal of oneness in mind, it is wise to examine what can keep us from it. In the typical relationship, there are some obstacles to loving compromise. First, the desires of both parties must be known by both parties. If either party withholds information, compromise is impossible. Withholding information—whether with pure intent or as an adversary—is a serious obstacle to oneness.

I once knew a young husband who had two job offers, one in the hometown of his insecure little bride and one far away. Now a job is a partnership matter. It affects the unit, not just the applicant. The young man vaguely understood this, so when his wife apprehensively asked which offer he wanted to take, he said, "Well, it doesn't matter a whole lot.

MAN AND WOMAN: JOY IN ONENESS

You want to go home, don't you?" When she answered with a pleading "yes," he took that job.

As it happened it was the wrong job to take for reasons that the young man had suspected but had not voiced. It was bad for his career which in turn was bad for the family. But the greatest damage was more subtle. He hadn't been open about his desires, and because his wife *was* open, she became *in his mind* the responsible party for the decision. She was not, of course, but because he had not *actively* compromised he felt *passively* compromised. He went through day after hostile day feeling that she had her way and he was suffering for it. His resentment grew because it was "all her fault." Their adversary relationship grew and they lost the joy of oneness.

How different the situation could have been. If only they had openly expressed their preferences, they could have listed the pros and cons for each option and then prayerfully decided which option was best for the *unit* and then, having entered into the discussion without selfishness, both could have been equally committed to the decision. Perhaps the discussion would have uncovered some of the wife's misgivings about the new area and the husband could have—in return for her support in the move—made special arrangements regarding the house or neighborhood. That way both could have had some of what they wanted. But more importantly, *both would have shared responsibility for the decision,* and there would have been no resentment.

Because the husband had abdicated his responsibility by not openly discussing his feelings, he had laid the responsibility at his wife's feet. The result was that she resented having to take the responsibility and he resented not being "free."

Reluctance to take responsibility for one's desires is common among wives: "Whatever you say, dear." I use the above example only to show that it happens the other way around as well. But women often lay all responsibility at the feet of their husbands and then spend the rest of their lives complaining that they take it. Their husbands, on the other hand, feel responsibility for every wrong choice so keenly that they come to resent the source of that heavy load and become increasingly authoritative and hostile. The more "authoritative" they become—requiring their wives to submit to *their* will instead of the will of the Father—the less they follow the Father themselves. Followership, it is to be remembered, is not always following the example of what God *is,* but following his directions as to what he wants us to be. It is not our role to start a flood or burn a city. It is our role to love God and to love our neighbors as ourselves. In other words, we should not *play* God, just *obey* him. Since his will is sometimes hard to see, we should seek the Holy Ghost for help.

The Holy Ghost comes through righteousness and love. And compromise is a first step in understanding the will of God. Man cannot jump from hostility to revelation. He must climb step by loving step by living the two great commandments. Compromise is, after all, living the second great commandment —loving your partner as yourself.

The Lord's instructions to the Quorum of the Twelve can be applied to marriage. The promised blessings are the same:

> And every decision made by either of these quorums must be by the unanimous voice of the same; that is, every member in each quorum must be agreed to its decisions, in order to make their decisions of the same power or validity one with the other— ... Unless this is the case, their decisions are not entitled to the same blessings.... The decisions of these quorums, or either of them, are to be made in all righteousness, in holiness, and lowliness of heart, meekness and long suffering, and in faith, and virtue, and knowledge, temperance, patience, godliness, brotherly kindness and charity; *Because the promise is, if these things abound in them they shall not be unfruitful in the knowledge of the Lord.* (Doctrine and Covenants 107:27, 29-31; italics added.)

A second obstacle to loving compromise is a lack of realism in expectations. It is defeating to negotiate believing you can do or have everything. There are few no-sacrifice situations. Sacrifice, remember, brings forth the blessings of heaven. Resources are limited. Time is limited. You are limited. The very essence of compromise is *choice*. That should not be surprising, as choice is the vehicle for all spiritual growth, and oneness is the greatest spirituality.

I have a friend whom I consider to be the true Supermom. (For me, incidentally, that term does not mean someone who cans peaches, pears, and string beans, bakes bread, and makes a quilt, all by 9:00 A.M.) One of her daughters came to her with a dilemma shortly after she turned eight. She had been approached about joining Brownies and Bluebirds (the preliminary groups for Girl Scouts and Campfire Girls). It all sounded so exciting that she wanted to join both. She also took piano and dancing lessons, and she attended Primary and was involved in many other things, so her mother lovingly said, "You know, Jenny, you and your time are limited. There are only a certain number of things you can do."

The little girl said she knew that was true, but wondered how she could possibly decide what to do. The choice was too hard.

Her mother said, "Well, the way you make any choice is to decide what is most important." She told her about eternal values and about what would most please her Heavenly Father and ultimately bring her the most happiness. They made a list and decided that they could not do without Primary, because

Man and Woman: Joy in Oneness

Heavenly Father wanted her there. And they could not do without piano lessons, because that was something she would need all her life. And they went down the list and placed the things that she should not do without at the top of the list. They soon saw that she had no time for Brownies or Bluebirds.

Compromise comes about when both parties understand that time and people are limited, and so they have to choose. Slowly, in the spirit of eternal progression, compromise is training for oneness.

8

Seeking the Good

One day long ago I made a long-distance phone call to tell my family that I was engaged to be married. The next week I received a treasured letter from my wise older brother.

Most divorces, he told me, are for one reason: somebody thinks he is giving too much, and it's not worth it to him because he feels he is getting little in return. But giving, he said, is what marriage is all about. It is an experiment in godhood, and godhood is pure service. If you don't like giving, then marriage is not for you. And your Father in heaven sees you. If you don't show him that you *like* being a wife and mother, he won't trouble you with that role in the eternities.

That letter started me on a long road toward understanding that celestialization is a process more than a reward. We spend our entire mortal estate making the choices that show our Father in heaven what we really want. Through our choices we become what we want to be. And then, when the end comes, we *are* what we have shown our Heavenly Father that we like being.

The choices come in little doses, more in inclinations than commitments. A small blessing comes, and we appreciate it so much we use it wisely and gratefully. Soon the blessing is added upon, and as we nurture the larger blessing, it grows too. The reverse is also true. Like a hidden talent, an unappreciated, discarded blessing will be taken away.

Our choices show what we value. We can have anything we want if we value it enough to pay the price to receive it. And if we value the small blessings, we will receive the greater. The key, then, to showing appreciation for our blessings and thereby watching them grow is to *see* their value. Faith is defined by Paul as the *substance* of things hoped for, the *evidence* of things not seen. (Hebrews 11:1.) We are not asked to hope in a vacuum. We are asked to look for evidence and substance and to *work* from those positive observations.

A wicked generation seeks after a sign, but a righteous one sees signs in all of life. A person in an adversary relationship dares the one who loves him to prove that love and puts up obstacles to make proof difficult. A person in a loving relationship sees love in many small things, has his proof, and directs his effort to the joy of the lover.

Seeking the Good

My husband often forgets birthdays and anniversaries. When we were first married, I believed that if he cared for me he would remember these holidays. So whenever such an occasion arose I made it tough for him to remember. If I got a greeting card from another family member, I hid it; if a friend called, I didn't let him know. And when midnight had passed, I announced almost gleefully, "Well, you forgot! I knew you would. You just don't care." In those days I never even noticed that he had worried about fixing the car before I had to take a trip in it, or quietly gone out to buy me some aspirin because I said I had a headache. Because I did not look for the evidence of his love, I did not see its substance. And because I did not see its substance, I had no faith in it. And because I had no faith in it, I didn't appreciate how hurt he would be to fall short in my eyes.

Now I have changed. I know he loves me and wants to make me happy but that dates are a problem for him. So I make sure in subtle ways that he knows that a special date is coming. I have eliminated the adversary relationship in this regard. I have sought and found the beauty of his love instead of fearing that love is not there. By looking for the good, not dwelling on the bad, I have opened myself to some beautiful blessings and given him the joy of being part of my holidays.

Man and Woman: Joy in Oneness

An old but oft-forgotten secret of human relationships is to look for the good in others and ignore the bad. Looking for the bad will send you into a world of separateness where there is no joy.

A line of Robert Browning's says it well:

> Where the apple reddens
> Never pry—
> Lest we lose our Edens,
> Eve and I. ("A Woman's Last Word," st. 5.)

Seek and find love in every blessing, whether great or small. As in all principles of partnership, if you cannot recognize love from others, and especially from your mate, you cannot recognize it from your Father in heaven. And if you cannot respond to love by accepting the righteous goals of others as your own, neither can you respond to the goals of your God. "Dream beautiful dreams," President Kimball said, "and then work to make those dreams come true." I might add: For where you show him your dreams are, there will your future be also.

9

Loving When Alone

Probably one of life's most painful frustrations is to desire oneness, to be ready and eager to leave off separateness, and yet to be single or to be in partnership with someone who treasures separateness above oneness. Even worse is to feel rejected in divorce when you have tried to be a good partner.

But none of us is married all his life, and "this life is the time . . . to prepare to meet God." (Alma 34:32.) This does not mean just the married years of this life, be they many, few, or non-existent.

But preparing is sometimes easier in a good marriage, because there is help when we falter. But it *is* possible to learn these lessons while going it alone. Rejecting joy and succumbing to misery is just as common in matrimony as in single life—maybe even more so.

I offer no magic formula for finding a mate or for enticing the mates we have into the first difficult steps of compromise to bring about the joy in oneness. But this I know: unless we use this life to learn to leave off our own separateness, we will not be prepared for celestial life. Unless we eliminate the adversary relationship in our dealings, accept the responsibility of making ourselves worthy, examine our motivation instead of searching for fulfillment, and take on the mission of the Savior to bring to pass the immortality and eternal life of man, the godly joy of eternal partnership will never be ours. We simply will not be ready for it.

Elder Boyd K. Packer has said that even if a woman cannot get her husband to church, she can get the church to her husband. So it is with the principles of partnership. With patience, long-suffering, and love unfeigned, we must enter into whatever golden moments of partnership are available.

Whether married or single, if we prepare to meet God, the eternal result will be the same. All of us are using this life to prepare for celestial family life or to reject it.

Some who have understood the value of service have not understood the importance of oneness. For example, Sir Francis Bacon said in response to questions about the single state: "It is difficult to water the world when you have a well to fill at home."

I would change that sentiment to: "It may be preferable to have the joy of filling a well at home,

Loving When Alone

but you can keep the living waters flowing if you get busy and water the world."

Whether we have a loving partner to learn these things with us, or whether we must learn alone, the important thing is that, if we will, we can find the joy in oneness.

If we decide to prepare, the road need not be an unhappy one. We will find great rewards in the little bits of partnership we enter into as we share the Savior's love with others. Living the gospel of love and agency is an individual responsibility.

10

The Joy in Oneness

Recently on a business trip, I attended sacrament meeting in an unfamiliar ward. An elderly man bore his testimony that day. He was gray and wrinkled, experienced and wise. "I am a child of God," he said, "as young as any tiny toddler, as I will soon go running up to my heavenly parents. I know my need to grow and to become what they want me to be. I am still looking to them and to my brothers and sisters for an example and pray that I might recognize the examples that I should follow."

I was overwhelmed by the insight that old man gave me about what it means to become as a little child. It means responding to love by wanting to be what He who loves me most would want me to be. It means seeking, recognizing, and following the right example. Lately I have shared the vision of this elderly child of God. I can readily see myself as a toddler at the knee of a loving teacher. The advan-

THE JOY IN ONENESS

tage I have over a real toddler is the choice of who my heroes will be.

In the scriptures, I have found a hero—the Apostle Paul.

Paul knew the joy of oneness. He was not protective of his own customs or interests. "I am made all things to all men," he said, "that I might by all means save some." (1 Corinthians 9:22.) And "saving some" was the overriding purpose in his life. It was also the Savior's purpose, and Paul, in his love for the Savior, shared it completely. Paul's letters show his enthusiasm at having found the path to joy. Most of them were written to convince others to find it too.

I have counted more than one hundred verses in his fourteen short letters admonishing the Saints to be unified that they might find joy. He tells them what to do (be one), how to do it (through service and love, or charity), and what the results will be (peace and glory):

> Now I beseech you, brethren, by the name of our Lord Jesus Christ, that ye all speak the same thing, and that there be no divisions among you; but that ye be perfectly joined together in the same mind and in the same judgment. (1 Corinthians 1:10.)

> There is neither Jew nor Greek, there is neither bond nor free, there is neither male nor female: for ye are all one in Christ Jesus. (Galatians 3:28.)

Man and Woman: Joy in Oneness

> He which soweth sparingly shall reap also sparingly; and he which soweth bountifully shall reap also bountifully. Every man according as he purposeth in his heart, so let him give; not grudgingly, or of necessity: for God loveth a cheerful giver. (2 Corinthians 9:6-7.)

> Bear ye one another's burdens, and so fulfil the law of Christ. (Galatians 6:2.)

> That he would grant you, according to the riches of his glory, to be strengthened with might by his Spirit in the inner man; that Christ may dwell in your hearts by faith; that ye, being rooted and grounded in love, may be able to comprehend with all saints what is the breadth and length, and depth, and height; and to know the love of Christ, which passeth knowledge, that ye might be filled with all the fulness of God. (Ephesians 3:16-19.)

I pray that we will have this fulness. By knowing the godlike role of being one with our mates and with others, we can be one with our Heavenly Father.

Index

Adversary relationship: in example of seminary class, 6-8; overcoming, in example of Y.W. committee, 8-9; is tool of Satan, 9-10; in being used instead of being useful, 12; eliminated through service, 12-13; in "employee mentality," 19-20; from withheld information, 35-37; proving love in, 42-43; eliminating, 46
Ammon, 31-32
Attitudes concerning employment, 19-20

"Backing" into service, 22-24
Bacon, Sir Francis, 46
Bad, looking for, 44
Banquet, example of doctor's 28-29
Blessings, using, 42
Bluebirds, 39-40
Boy Scouts. *See* Scouting program, example of
Boys, ideas of, regarding girls, 16-18
Brownies, 39-40

Browning, Robert, 44
Bruton Parish Church, example of, 10-11

Celestialization, 41-42, 46
Child, becoming as little, 48
Choice, 38-42
Completeness, 2-3
Compromise: necessary to achieve oneness, 33; definition of, 34, 38; obstacles to, 35-40; is training for oneness, 40
Consecration, meaning of, 1-2

Dante, 21
Defensiveness, 8-9
Dependency (when forced upon others), 11-12
Divorce, 41, 45
Donne, John, 2

Eagle Scouts, 23-24
Education, 15-17
"Employee mentality," 19-21
English (for an education), 24-25
Excitement, looking for, 24

MAN AND WOMAN: JOY IN ONENESS

Expectations, unrealistic, 38-40

Faith, 42

Family: as related to celestial kingdom, 4; rejection of partnership principles in, 4-5; filling, goals, 27, 30-32; caring for different responsibilities as, 28-29; separateness in, 28-30; compared to corporation, 34-35

Finding: ourselves, 14-16, 22; fulfillment, 22-25

Followership, 37-38

Fulfillment: cannot come from separateness, 1; comes through service, 14-15; does not come from recognition, 22-24; from wanting and investing, 24; from college education, 24-25; from working toward family goals, 30-32

Girls, attractiveness in, 17-18

Giving, 41, 50

Goals: setting lofty, 21-22; achieving family, 26-32; reconciling family and vocational, 28-29; writing down family, 30-31; awareness of each other's, 30-31

God, 37-38, 45-46, 50

Good, seeking, 41-44

Haight, David B., 33

Heroes, choosing, 48-49

Holy Ghost, 34, 37-38

Homes, caring for, 26-28

Husband: becoming a good, 17-18; example of first doctor, 28-29; example of second doctor, 29-30; authoritative, 37; example of forgetful, 43

Information, withholding, 35-36

Jesus Christ, 3, 47, 49-50

Job offers, example of man with two, 35-37

Joy: from partnership with God, 2; Christ wants our, 3; absence of, 4-5; of oneness, 9, 49; service brings, 12; oneness brings, 16, 24; *suffer* antonym for, 19; in oneness, 33, 45-50; losing, of oneness, 35-36; directing effort to, of loved ones, 42; separateness has no, 44; rejecting, 45; of eternal partnership, 46; we can find, in oneness, 46-47; path to, 49; Paul on, 49-50

Kimball, Spencer W., 34, 44

Lamoni, 31

Lamoni's father, 31-32

Letter from brother, 41

Love: significance of, 3-4; as principle of partnership, 3-5; in example of Y.W. committee member, 8-9; neighbor as yourself, 38; in adversary or loving relationships, 42; in example of forgetful husband, 43; seeking, 43-44;

INDEX

when alone, 45-47; sharing, of Savior, 47; responding to, of God, 48

Man, example of elderly, 48
Marriage: as purpose of life, 1; difficult but necessary, 4-5; example of separateness in, 28-29; instructions to Quorum of Twelve applied to, 38; based on giving, 41; helps prepare us, 45
Mates, finding and helping, 45-46
McGinley, Phyllis, 17
Mothers must be educated, 15-17
Motivation, 25, 46

Nurse (in example of doctor's wife), 28-29

Obedience, chain of, 34
Oneness: defined as partnership, 1; based on love, 2-4; joy lost when, is rejected, 4-5; love is joy of, 8-9; contributing to, 15-16; refusing, 20-21; based on wanting to contribute, 24; not achieved overnight, 33; obstacles to goal of, 35-40; when single, 45-47; importance of, 46; of Saints, 49; with Heavenly Father, 50
Openness in families, 35-37
Order in a home, 26-28

Packer, Boyd K., 46

Partners, becoming worthy, 14-18
Partnership: with God, 1-2; based on love, 3; based on service, 4; principles of, difficult to learn, 4-5; loss of, from hostility, 10-11; eternal, 46; entering into, 46
Paul, 49-50
Pope, Alexander, 2
Preparing for God and celestial family, 45-47
President: stake Young Women's, 8-9; of a marriage, 34-35
"Presiding" officer, 34-35
Primary, 26-27, 39-40
Principles of partnership, 1-5, 33-34
Propensity to unite, 2-3
Purpose of our existence, 1-2

Quorum of Twelve, 38

Realism in expectations, 38-40
Recognition, 22-24
Relief Society class, example of, 26-28
Respect for each other, 16-18
Responsibility, 14, 26-28, 35-38, 46
Role, accepting our, 21

Sacrifice, 38-40
Scouting program, example, of, 22-24
Scoutmaster, 23-24
Scripture chase, example of, 6-8
Seeing ourselves and others, 19, 42-44
Self-esteem, 26-28

53

MAN AND WOMAN: JOY IN ONENESS

Self-pity, 10-11
Seminary class, 6-8
Separateness: is not our purpose, 1; overcoming, 8-9; in example of doctor and wife, 28-29; when single, 45-47; leaving off, 46
Service: as principle of partnership, 4-5; considered as dirty word, 11-12; definition of, 12-13; is way to eliminate adversary relationship, 13; developing ourselves for, 15-16; outside of home, 26-28; of Paul, 49; how to do, 49-50
Servitude, 11-12
Shakespeare, appreciating, 24-25
Single, being, 1, 45-47
Smith, George Albert, 15
Supermom, example of, 39-40

Teilhard De Chardin, Pierre, 2-3
Testimony of elderly man, 48

Tour of Bruton Parish Church, 10-11

Unity, working in, 19-21

Wife: example of doctor's, 28-29; example of King Lamoni's, 31; example of Lamoni's father's, 31-32; example of insecure, 35-37; example of, who could not see husband's love, 43
Wives: those who do not become, 1, 45-47; must be educated, 17-18; taking second place to husband's work, 28-29; reluctance to take responsibility among, 37
Woman, example of sick, 29-30
Women, importance of, 10-11, 17

Young, Brigham, 17
Young Women's committee, example of, 8-9